WRITE A LETTER

WRITE A LETTER

Put Pen to Paper and Put a Smile on
the Face of a Stranger, a Friend or Yourself

JODI ANN BICKLEY

PENGUIN BOOKS

PENGUIN BOOKS

UK | USA | Canada | Ireland | Australia
India | New Zealand | South Africa

Penguin Books is part of the Penguin Random House group of companies
whose addresses can be found at global.penguinrandomhouse.com.

Penguin
Random House
UK

First published 2018

001

Copyright © Jodi Ann Bickley, 2018

The moral right of the author has been asserted

Printed in Italy by L.E.G.O. S.p.A.
A CIP catalogue record for this book is available from the British Library

ISBN: 978–0–241–98469–7

www.greenpenguin.co.uk

To my girls, Dylan and Dotty.
May you always believe in magic and the
power of your words.

Acknowledgements

Firstly, to my team: Sam, Dylan and Dotty, who however lost at sea I get always provide the brightest of lights to guide me home. My mum, for instilling in me the power of my words to not only help ourselves but to try and help the world around us. To Jack and Emily at Penguin for believing in the magic of letters and letting me put this book together; it has been therapeutic and an absolute joy working with you. To Hannah, Christine H and my handful of letter writers who are slowly but surely helping me get through the 12,000 letter requests in the One Million Lovely Letters inbox. The project could not keep going without you and it's a privilege to have you in my little team. And finally to everybody who has engaged with One Million Lovely Letters, whether it has been requesting a letter, reading the book or talking to me on social media – I get to write letters every day because of you and that is incredible and something I am forever thankful for. Words are extremely powerful and sometimes all it takes is a few to remind someone that they are loved and they aren't on their own, and hopefully I get to do that for all of my days. Thank you so much for reading and engaging with this book – I hope you've felt the magic too.

Introduction

Writing letters has been pretty important in my life. In fact, letters are so important to me that I want to get you writing them, sharing them with others and, in turn, getting them to write letters, too. I want the whole world to start writing to each other. Why? Because I truly believe that it's the best way to communicate with friends, family, neighbours, people you've never met, people who don't exist, the world around you, animals, the past and yourself.

Writing a letter might seem strange, or old-fashioned. But it needn't be. This book is going to show you how to incorporate letters into your world and gain pleasure, solace or the release of emotion you've needed. It has everything that you need to start. In fact, we can start right now!

Throughout this book there are going to be prompts to write to people – all kinds of different people. Sometimes I'll ask you to write to somebody more than once in the hope that you can strike up a back-

and-forth; sometimes one will just open up naturally. Sometimes I'll recommend that you write to something imaginary, or a place within you, or to somebody, but with the knowledge that it's a letter you're never going to deliver. And you can be creative, too. These are suggestions and ideas, not commands. What's important is to get writing.

I'm going to start right now, with a letter to you.

Jodi Ann Bickley
Penguin Random House UK
80 Strand
London WC2R 0RL

Hi!

I'm Jodi Ann Bickley, I'm twenty-nine and I live with my husband and two children in a tall, colourful house in Kings Heath, Birmingham. My stomach still flips when I write 'husband and children', part fizz and happiness and part disbelief that I'm not sixteen any more. I often feel as though I'm an imposter – a child in my mum's high heels. I make a lovely apple crumble and I put the milk into a cup of tea first, which bothers almost everyone that has ever known me. I worry about everything; you can find me at 4 a.m., worrying about whether I looked at somebody the wrong way in Year 8. But I'm working on it. I'm hoping, one day, my worries can be contained to the last five years instead of the last fifteen.

Letters have always been a HUGE part of my life. I'm the girl who kept every silly little note passed in class and every super-important love letter in a big box under the bed. Now I write letters to people all over the world via my project One Million Lovely Letters, which I started five years ago. Back then, I needed a lighthouse to guide me out of a dark place. I've battled with depression since I was sixteen and after a period of long-term illness it had become all-consuming. My letters became a way for me to start the climb back up from the bottom and with each one I write it's like another step towards the place I want to be. My letters help me cope, fill me with joy and act as a form of therapy. I hope that it's the same for the people who write to me. And this is why I'm so excited about this project: I want to share the gift of writing with you.

I hope that this book brings you the same happiness my letters bring me. I hope you get the words out that you've needed to and that you let people know just how much you feel for them. Letters are real-life magic; they snapshot a moment in time and can be treasured for ever.

I hope you have fun, learn something about yourself and send some really beautiful letters out into the world (or to be kept in a box, under your bed). You can start by writing to me. I'm going to collect all the letters I receive from this project and put them in a box, but also up online, at https://www.instagram.com/jodiannbickley. I hope you send me beautiful, exciting things, so that we can make a little corner of the internet a special place.

This brings me on to the book you're reading. You'll notice it's sort of unusual. The first half is here to help you be inspired to WRITE A LETTER. But the second half is there to actually get you writing. You'll find beautiful paper that you can easily tear out – I thought it would be more helpful if you had the paper right here rather than having to go out and get some. Use the stub that is left behind to keep a record of who you wrote to. Then, once you've finished writing, you can stick your letter in an envelope and send it. Or, if you don't have any envelopes, simply fold the paper in half, seal it across the top with tape, and voilà! a DIY postcard.

Write the address, stick on a stamp and send it to me. My publishers' address is at the top of this letter and they will pass them on to me. You'll also find a flap in the back of this book. Use it to save all the letters you'll receive in return. When you've completed this project I hope you'll keep writing to people who've written to you. I think the best thing about sending letters is the hope that you'll receive something in return.

Jodi x

to the teacher who inspired you

Write a letter to the teacher who inspired you, whether it is to speak up or to pursue a certain subject – write to them and let them know what their actions led to. I'm going to write to my primary-school headteacher, Mrs Penman. I'd been bullied at my previous school and I arrived at Yorkmead Primary with no confidence and in lots of broken pieces. Over the next three years she built me up and stuck me back together. I headed off to secondary school as someone who didn't fear school but actually really enjoyed it. Imagine how different your life would be without that special teacher – write to them!

Tick me once you've completed each letter! ⮞

to your mum

Our relationships with our parents can be complex. Sometimes they are incredible; sometimes they can be incredibly difficult. Sometimes they can be non-existent. My mum has always been my constant; when everything else has felt like it was crumbling, my mum has been my rock. She's my best friend, and I feel completely indebted to her for being a never-ending source of love, strength and inspiration. Write a letter to your mum, explaining how you feel about her and what role she has played in your life and who you've turned out to be.

Dear Mum,

I've tried to write this letter ten times. It's absolutely impossible. There are not enough words to express my gratitude, love and appreciation for you. In the darkest storms you've turned up with an umbrella and wellies and waded through the rain to me. You've never allowed me to face a battle alone and I couldn't have got through them without you. As a mum, you've been the most incredible one there could be. The only thing better has been watching you become a nanny. The girls and I are so lucky to have you, and we will be here with our wellies and umbrellas, ready to dance in the rain or wade through the storms whenever you need us. For ever.

See, never enough words.

Jodi x

to a stranger

So, you've written to me – thanks! But what's your perfect introduction? The great thing about letters is that you have a chance to think about what you're going to say before you say it. So, imagine the perfect introduction to you – what would it say? Write a letter doing just that: introduce yourself to a stranger and explain who you are, where you're from and where you want to go. If you're feeling brave, give it to somebody. Letters can be a great way to make new friends.

to say 'thank you'

You can never say 'thank you' enough. It's always appreciated. Who in your life are you grateful for and why? Write a letter of gratitude to someone. This one's really hard for me, because there are so many people to say thank you to. Still, I hope these prompts are causing you to think about all the people in your life you can write to. With a prompt like this, maybe you might want to send more than one letter; maybe there are a lot of people you want to thank. It's always best said with a letter.

WRITE A LETTER...

to your neighbour

There's nothing better than feeling part of a community, but a recent survey shows us that over 50 per cent of people here in Britain don't even know any of our neighbours' names. Let's rectify that. Write a letter to your neighbour. Maybe you could invite them round for a cup of tea or offer to feed the cat if they go on holiday.

to a friend

Throughout this book I'm going to give you a little nudge from time to time to try and keep up regular exchanges with two people in your life. 'Leyla' is a friend who you adore but no longer lives close enough to have a cup of tea and a catch-up with. And 'Nancy' is an older person – maybe a relative or somebody in your neighbourhood. Somebody who might be lonely, for instance, and from whom you could learn a lot about life, somebody who may have solutions to things going on in yours. These are just suggestions, though. Write to who you want to write to. But try your best to do it regularly, and make sure that, if you get a response, you always write back! First one, then, write to your friend and tell them what's been going on since you last saw them. More importantly, ask them what's going on with them.

to an incredible doctor

When I first became ill with Chronic Fatigue Syndrome (CFS), nobody could work out what was going on. I had test after test to try and find some reason behind why I was so poorly. When we finally found out, I was sent to an incredible doctor called Kim. She not only explained what was happening to me but validated the pain I was struggling with. Like many illnesses, CFS is invisible to the outside world. I at last felt heard and understood, and it was such a relief. Has there been a doctor that has gone above and beyond for you, helped you or a friend or family member with a long-term problem, or simply given you the medicine you needed when you needed it? Write them a letter to let them know how you're feeling now you're better.

to your favourite musician

Music can evoke emotion like nothing else; it can take us back to an exact moment, an exact feeling – whether it was magical or heartbreaking. Music is extremely powerful and the people who create it are very special indeed. I plan to write to Adele. I first heard her on Myspace when I was sixteen: an internet friend had posted a video of her singing in his living room, and I was instantly in awe. Ever since, her music has provided the perfect soundtrack to all my romantic highs and lows. When I felt like I'd had enough of love and I was destined for a life pushing dressed-up cats around in a pram, it was Adele's music that both comforted me and gave me the confidence to open myself up to love again. Write to your favourite musician, the one who can transport you like no other. It's really easy to find the best address on the internet. Adele, for instance, is at:

Adele
XL Recordings
1 Codrington Mews
London W11 2EH

to your favourite writer

There is nothing better than getting lost in a good book. I can get so engrossed in a story or a poem or a play, I never want it to end. And when it does I spend all my time looking forward to the moment when I can immerse myself once again. So, write a letter to your favourite writer, telling them just how they make you feel. It's easy to find out where to write to. Most books will have the name of the publisher, and a simple search on the internet will provide their address. For instance, you've already written to me once, but if you want to write again, I'm at:

Jodi Ann Bickley
Penguin Random House UK
80 Strand
London WC2R 0RL

To Zia Ahmed,

As a fan of your work, I'll forever be in awe of the way you craft your message, as a poem or a story. It's unlike anything else I've ever read or heard. Your voice is so important, with the current state of the world. You make complex, difficult issues into something accessible and beautiful for your readers and listeners. That's a skill that not many have, and I'm not sure you realize just how incredible your work is. Please, never, ever stop. Your ability to evoke feeling and to paint a picture with your words is totally unique. You need to be heard, by everybody.

Thank you,
Jodi x

to your fifteen-year-old self

If you knew then what you know now, what would you say? Use the power of hindsight to write a letter to your younger self. Try and give yourself the wisdom then that you have now. Write to yourself as you were when you were fifteen years old. This is my version.

To Jodi,

When that one boy with a skateboard calls you 'fat', walk away. Don't give him space, physically or mentally; otherwise, you will forever give words like his the room to grow. And they don't deserve it. Your body is beautiful and it's yours — it doesn't need validation from others. Treat it kindly, feed it often and love it unconditionally. It's going to take you dancing until sunrise, fighting battles big and small, and will finally go on to provide two of the most amazing little people this world has to offer. Education isn't going to be the route for you, but keep writing — write everything down, because it all matters. Keep a diary. You always say you're going to and give up in March. Get through a year, and then another and another. Write letters, tell people how you feel, let them know what they mean to you. Please stop worrying about tomorrow, next week and next year. Focus on now — it is all that we have and worrying about what's next will only steal you away from that. Know that you never have to shrink any part of you to make yourself worthy, whether it is your personality or stomach — all that you are, exactly as you are, will always be enough.

Be kind to yourself,
Jodi

to your future self

You've written to your past, but what do you hope for the future? Right now, how would you like your life to turn out? Check in with your future self by writing them a letter.

to someone who has made an impact

Write to someone who has made a social statement, maybe a celebrity or someone who has made an impact by standing up to somebody. Two examples for me would be Emma Gonzalez, a high-school senior who survived the Stoneman Douglas High School shooting in Parkland, Florida. She co-founded the gun control advocacy group Never Again and helped organize the nationwide March for Our Lives. Celebrity-wise, I'd write to Jameela Jamil, who has started a movement called I-weigh after becoming disheartened with the amount of focus put on women and their weight. With I-weigh, she wrote her weight in what she is made up of – 'friendships, a loving relationship, a successful career' – and this caught on. Now hundreds if not thousands of women have joined in and felt empowered by the movement. Tell them that you care.

to make someone laugh

This letter doesn't have to be particularly long or profound; it just has to be funny. Write a letter to anybody. But you have to make them laugh.

to your granddad

The thing I remember most clearly about my granddad is that he smelled like spearmint chews and cigars, he looked like the BFG and he made me feel completely safe whenever he was around. Write a letter to your granddad, letting him know how he makes you feel.

to a place that is special to you

An old house, a holiday destination, a school or a place where you fell in love – write to somewhere that will always be special to you and leave it there. If your place comes from a once-in-a-lifetime holiday and you can't leave it there, perhaps you could keep your letter in a safe place along with another memento – a photograph, say.

To Subculture (every Saturday night at the Carling Academy, Birmingham, between 2004 and 2007). Four girls clutching hands, hoping the extra eyeliner and low lighting would convince the bouncer we were eighteen. Thankfully, it always did. While we turned eighteen on your dance floor, it wasn't until two years later that Subculture was firmly our stomping ground and we became adults. We fell in love over green drinks and pop punk and swore those nights would never be beaten. In many ways, they still can't be. That's because it was here that we grew up, alongside our best friends, and no matter how much time passes, however old we become, I will always be that girl, dancing to those songs, wearing that eyeliner.

Thanks for the memories, Subculture.
Jodi

to someone you appreciate

Some people go to work every day and aren't appreciated. Perhaps the job brings upset to some, or perhaps it's a job not considered as desirable by cruel people – but somebody has to do it. Your local traffic warden or your local dustbin man (I love mine!) – write them a little note to say thanks. Give it to them. Let them know they are appreciated.

to your dad

My dad has never been around – well, never long enough for me to form any sort of relationship with him. It's not really felt like a sore point with me, though. I guess, to me, the concept of a Dad has always felt mythical – like goblins or unicorns. It's the loveliest feeling seeing my husband with our girls, because I'm getting to experience that fatherly bond for the first time and, although it is as a spectator, it's the most beautiful thing. Please use the space at the end of this book to write a letter to your dad. Let him know how you feel about him and the role he has played in your life and where you've ended up.

Hey, Dad,

It's weird writing 'Dad'. I don't think I've ever used that term out loud to address you. It almost feels like a word from a foreign language. For all the years I haven't known you, there hasn't been a part of me that sincerely ever wanted to. There have been moments, fleeting ones, where I wonder if we would get on or whether I get any of my personality traits from you, but never a time I've felt like there is a space where you would fit.

I don't look on in envy at other people with their fathers or lust after the idea of father–daughter dances. I had all I needed in a male role model in the newsreader Trevor McDonald. He wasn't family, but he turned up every night at six o'clock to tell me about the day, and that was enough. Basically, what I'm trying to say is, don't worry about it. I'm not sitting here missing you, I haven't missed out on that part of my life and I don't resent you for not turning up either. I have a pretty amazing mum that forever turns up, loves me fiercely and has never made me feel like I was missing out on another parent. Which has done you great favours really: there isn't an adult girl walking around missing her dad because I simply never had one to miss.

I hope you're well,
Jodi

to an older person

Start a correspondence with Nancy, who we discussed on page 13! Over half of people aged seventy-five and over live alone, and two-fifths of all older people (around 3.9 million) say that the television is their main source of company (Age UK, 2014). If you don't know any older people, or there aren't any you can reach out to, perhaps you could write to one of the many charities who can put you in touch with older people through writing, for instance Age Concern (https://www.ageuk.org.uk) or the Jo Cox Foundation (https://www.jocoxfoundation.org). Remember, this is just a suggestion: the important thing is to strike up a conversation with somebody; it doesn't really matter who they are.

to a prisoner

All over the world there are people who are incarcerated; some have done awful, evil things but some are behind bars simply because of who they choose to love or what they believe in. Here, I want you to write a letter to a prisoner. There are lots of ways to write to somebody who is in prison. Check out Amnesty International's campaign Write for Rights, where you can be put in touch with somebody who has been imprisoned because of who they love, what they believe or what they think.

to your first crush

My first crush is the one that hurt me the least and felt the most like a Disney film, so it will forever be my favourite of all. Write to your first crush. Let them know what you think of them now and how that first-crush experience set you up for a life in love.

To Liam,

From the moment you made fun of me in front of the whole gymnasium I was hooked. Of course I was – I was eleven. Whatever that first encounter was, against all odds, we became the best of friends. The odds being you liked football and r'n'b whereas I was into punk rock (and Busted) and had colourful jewellery up to my elbows. It doesn't seem like much now – but at the time we may as well have been chalk and cheese. What we learned over the next five years is that we were actually very similar and what developed was an immense friendship and the knowledge that we both thought the other was pretty wonderful. Classes were spent writing I ♡ on my hand in the prettiest gel pens and lunch breaks trying to catch your eye from across the playground. Night was spent on MSN messenger, changing screen names to various song lyrics in the hope you'd find yourself in them. There are plenty of cringe moments to that five-year crush, but I wouldn't change a second of it. It was magic! It all came together in an awkward kiss at our Year 11 prom to Robbie Williams's 'She's the One', and that was enough. Anything more would have ruined it. For what it was, it was really perfect. We didn't really keep in contact after school – life happens, and you lose people way too quickly. Only later in life do you realize you would have really liked to have seen how they turned out. Wherever you are, whatever you're doing, I hope you're happy.

Thanks for the magic!
Jodi

to your best friend

There is one person who gets you more than anybody else in the world. You've laughed with them, cried with them, your best memories are those where they are by your side, and you have secrets that only they will ever know. Write a letter to your best friend letting them know why having them in your world makes it that much more wonderful.

to a child

Whether you have children, would like them one day or couldn't imagine anything worse (in which case, if you didn't want to write to the children you don't want, maybe you could write to a child that you love – a niece or nephew, a little cousin), this is a letter for them. What would you like to say, what would you like them to know about the world and what do you hope for them?

To my girls,

My beautiful little women, you bring so much happiness to this world and I will forever be in awe of you both. I want you to know that everything you are has always and will always be enough. Never feel you have to change to fit somebody else's vision of what you should be. All you should be is yourselves, unapologetically – loudly, wildly, but always kindly. Kindness is so important. Throw it around wherever you go because it is always, always, needed. Think before you speak but never censor what you're saying because you feel that it won't be heard or that it isn't valid. What you have to say is as important as what anyone else has to say. Always make sure it comes from a place of love and truth. There are bad people in this world, baby girls, but there are also shining lights, people who will amaze you and inspire you and make you laugh. Find them, surround yourself with them, because you deserve them, their love and their magic. However beautiful your heels look, always take a pair of flats with you too – your feet will thank you. Don't drink anything that is blue. Know that you can never die from a hangover or from heartbreak, however much it feels like you will at the time. Don't let the actions of one partner stop you from throwing yourself into love: your heart is resilient and you deserve all of those movie moments to counter the heart grazes that will come. Look after each other, call just to say I love you and send a care package whenever it's needed. It's the tiny things that count for pretty much everything in life. The little moments, the snapshots, the blink of an eye – that's where the magic lies.

Stay curious.
Stay wild.
Stay wonderful.

I love you,
Mummy x

to someone you've lost touch with

Sometimes, life happens and you lose touch with someone who you later wish you'd held on to a little tighter. While I was at university in Manchester (albeit only for a couple of months) I met a handful of people who I truly loved. I'd gone to university on a whim, thinking I had to, thinking my life lacked direction, and I realized pretty instantly I didn't belong there. What made those few months bearable were the people I met, the fun we had and the moments we shared. Now we are spectators to each other's lives via social media and, although I haven't seen them for the longest time, I treasure them and the friendship we had. Write a letter to somebody you've lost touch with, because social media just isn't the same.

to make someone's day

How's Leyla? What is she up to? Have you noticed anything on social media recently? Has she made an announcement that you feel deserves a written correspondence, a congratulations or a message of love and support? A letter can make all the difference and make someone's day.

to say sorry

Whether it's something small like getting coffee granules in the sugar pot or something a lot more serious, saying sorry is appreciated. Although it can't fix everything, it can act as a bridge to build on. Write a letter to someone to say that you're sorry. And really mean it.

to your nan

I love a nan! Although my lovely nan died when I was really young, I have adopted other people's grandparents along the way as my own. They are full of stories, wisdom and wit. A nan is a treasure trove – write to yours and let her know what she's taught you and why you think she's great.

to tell the truth

Honesty is the best policy, right? Well, sometimes it can be a little tricky facing the truth. Write an honest letter to someone and tell them something you need to. You don't have to send it but do get it down on paper. Remember: better out than in.

to remember an amazing day

Ever wish you could have bottled that day you felt amazing, the day you really believed in yourself or felt incredible? Write it down for you to open on a day when you're feeling not so wonderful.

to the last person you kissed

The last person I kissed was a friend in passing; we hadn't seen each other for a while but we both had screaming toddlers and stopping in the middle of a crowded high street wasn't an option. I'm going to write to her to catch up, to tell her all the things I wanted to tell her and find out the things I wanted to find out that couldn't be said because life is just too busy. Slow down and write a letter to the last person you kissed.

to encourage!

Write a letter to encourage! Whether it be to a friend who has a dream that they don't think they are capable of achieving or to someone who has been putting something off because they find it difficult, maybe they need to speak up about something at work or quit a habit. Be there for them and let them know you believe in them!

to tell someone they are incredible

Whether it's your boss, your teacher or someone else in authority, write to let them know how incredibly they're doing. It's so important to stick up for others, and it's important to make sure that those in authority don't forget that you're all part of a team. Failing that, if you're feeling extra confident, let this authority figure know why you think you're an asset.

to someone you've been meaning to write to

It's been nagging at you. You've been meaning to write it down for a while now, but you haven't had the time. Or maybe you couldn't find the right words. Perhaps it's left unfinished in a drawer somewhere, or perhaps you've scrunched up a couple of drafts already. Write the letter you've been meaning to write, to the person you've been meaning to send it to.

to tell someone you are grateful

It's the tiny things that count. Write a letter to somebody thanking them for a small act of kindness, whether it was a lovely cup of coffee, a text message that made your day or a hug when you needed it. Let them know that you're grateful.

to forgive yourself

We all have our dark corners where we store our doubts, fears, regrets, hang-ups and upsets. It can get pretty heavy if you let it, so use the space at the end of this book to write a letter forgiving yourself. Think about some of that excess baggage you carry and then let it go.

Hey,

I forgive myself for the hells that I've put myself through. For the times I didn't listen to my body's need to rest, to eat, to stop. I forgive myself for being hell-bent on destruction one too many times and the impact that had on the people around me. I forgive myself for the hangovers and for the fifty-plus times I've sworn it will never happen again and then it did. I forgive myself for the bad boys who became bad men and for putting myself in situations which were never going to end in anything other than trouble. I forgive myself for nearly giving up, for settling and thinking I was unworthy of happiness. I forgive myself for the terrible haircuts and the uncomfortable shoes. I forgive myself for the constant over-thinking, the what-ifs, and for going back over every argument, every text message and every social situation that has happened since the late nineties.

I forgive myself for taking this long to let go.

Jodi

to make a stranger's day

Write a lovely letter to a stranger – a letter of reassurance and love – and leave it somewhere for them to find: on the bus, in a library book or on a bench. I promise it will make their day.

To you,

I just need you to know that the pain you are feeling right now is temporary. Although now it feels all-encompassing, heavy and thick, you will reach the other side of it. I'm not saying it will be easy. Some days will be so, so tough but all I ask of you is to look back. Look back at all the times you weren't sure you'd make it. Look at all those mountains you've climbed and mud you've waded through. You made it through and those people you see in the shadows? Look to their feet. They have bright yellow welly boots and umbrellas in hand because you are never in the darkness alone. You are surrounded by people who love you, waiting to hold your hand whenever you need it; it is never a weakness to ask for help. It's so, so brave and the moment you do you'll see that the darkness is so much less scary and easier to navigate with someone by your side.

Love,
Jodi xx

to ask for advice

Did Nancy get back to you? I think the great thing about older people is that they have so much to teach us, so much experience and wisdom. If you're writing to an older person, draw on that wellspring of knowledge for advice, counsel and care. Perhaps you have a problem that you're trying to work through. Retired people have often been there, done that and bought the T-shirt. And remember: if you want to keep up a correspondence, always ask questions.

to console a friend

When life hands us the really awful bits, we need our friends and bucket-loads of love. A friend in need is a friend indeed. So write a letter to console a friend who's having a hard time and let them know that you're there for them.

to forgive someone

Being angry or upset by someone takes up a lot of space in your mind. It takes a lot of strength to be able to forgive someone for something they did and, although it won't change whatever it is you're forgiving them for having happened in the first place, you will be able to go into the future feeling lighter, without the heaviness of that feeling. Write a letter forgiving somebody.

to your first love

To love and be loved is an incredible feeling, especially your first love. The newness, the intensity and the fear – you will never feel that amazing ever again. I first fell in love with my husband at seventeen. We were sitting at Wythall train station in Worcestershire, sharing a bag of Liquorice Allsorts which we'd bought with some money a woman gave us for phoning her when we found her son's phone on the floor. I remember thinking in that moment that I didn't want to be anywhere else in the world and, although I'd thought people were awesome before, nobody got me like this person did and I could spend all my days with him and never get bored. Unfortunately, we never got to be boyfriend and girlfriend back then – it just wasn't our time. We lived our lives and loves and learned the lessons that we needed to so we could truly appreciate what we had when the universe threw us back in front of each other. And thank goodness it did. Write a letter to your first love.

To Sam,

There are moments when I look at you – when you're driving, playing with the girls or losing at Fifa (I'm sorry, I'll always be your biggest fan!) – and I become so conscious that my heart is in my chest. It sparkles in those moments, and that sounds so cheesy to write down, but if true love is actually a thing, I think that feeling is the signal. There is no other person I would rather try and be a grown-up with, laugh with when we feel like we're in way over our heads and high-five over the tiny victories. We fell in love as teenagers, went on to love others and live lives that somehow, thankfully, brought us right back to where we belong. You are home, and I can't wait for the rest of our adventures.

My love, best friend and team mate, you are incredible.

Jodi x

to the first person who broke your heart

At some point or another, we've all felt that our heart might fall out due to heartbreak and, if it did, it would probably be less painful than going through the experience of heartbreak itself. Probably. The first time's the worst, until the second and then the third, but each time you learn a little bit about yourself, which makes it worth it, right? Write a letter to the first person who broke your heart.

to your fears

What are you scared of? What is it about it that scares you? Did you experience something that terrified you, or is it just the sheer thought of it that's always scared you? For me, it's the concept of death – not my own but of the people I love. Aged eleven, I remember staying up for three nights running because I'd convinced myself that, if I fell asleep, I'd wake up and my mum would have died. It sounds grim, but it's always been a fear of mine and, at times, that can be pretty crippling. Write a letter to your fears, addressing them and trying to work them out. Once you write this letter, burn it, bin it or bury it.

to express your hopes

I remember being thirteen and lying in bed dreaming that, by the age of twenty-five I would be a journalist, married and living in New York. At the age of twenty-nine, I've achieved a little bit of that, though the dream of New York has been replaced with wanting a colourful house by the seaside and maybe a good night's sleep. Write a letter expressing all your hopes and dreams and pin it somewhere you can see it.

to someone you miss

You don't have to be out of touch with somebody to miss them. Whether it's a best friend who lives far away or some-one you wish you had held on to, let them know you miss having them by your side. My letter is to my best friend Alice. She lives in Bristol, which is only a train journey away, but the distant can sometimes feel like a whole different planet.

To Alice,

Of all the people on the planet, I have never met another one who I feel quite as comfortable with as you. We met at twelve, two awkward pre-teens in swimsuits waiting in the queue for the diving board. We sat on the edge and flung ourselves over, landing with a splash in the water. From that moment on, if we ever found ourselves in at the deep end, we'd be in it together. From the worst of heartbreaks to the incredible nights we swore we would never forget, we were always side by side. Even at our furthest apart, whether that's geographically or psychologically, I've always been wildly protective of our friendship and our way of always working back to each other. And we do, every time.

Love you always,
Jodi

to someone you may take for granted

Some people are just incredible, and we almost get used to it. It's just the way they are, so we don't feel the need to consistently say thank you every time they do something lovely. Well, superheroes sometimes need to hear that they're super too. Use the space at the end of this book to write a letter to someone you may take for granted.

To Fran,

I'd been hibernating for weeks after having Dotty – I've always been quite skilled in avoiding text messages and hiding from phone calls – but when you texted I replied instantly. There are certain people in the world who settle you, and you've always made the crazy bits of being a mum feel normal, as you are so open about your own experiences. You have never made me feel as though I'm being ridiculous. When you arrived at the front door with a cottage pie and the offer of watching the baby while I had a wash, I welled up, because that's exactly what I needed, a friend who got exactly how I was feeling. I didn't need flowers that I'd forget to water and go on to feel like a failure for killing, or chocolates to make me feel even more bloated post-baby – I just needed a mate, a pie and a shower.

Thanks for being great,
Jodi

to remind someone of their strength

From time to time, we can doubt ourselves. We forget how incredibly strong and resilient we are and need reminding. Write a letter to somebody reminding them of their strength.

to tell a friend you are thinking of them

How is Leyla? Did she enjoy your last letter? What's happening in her world? Find a card that sums your relationship up, whether it's the picture on the front or the sentiment inside, and let her know that you're thinking of her!

to the person who hurt you the most

Not all people are good; some can actually be pretty awful and affect us in ways that echo for a really long time and even change us completely. This one may be difficult, but also therapeutic: write a letter to the person who hurt you the most, for whatever reason. Again, you don't have to send it. You can rip it up, stomp on it or feed it to a wild boar, but get that experience – and get them – out of your system.

Dean,

For so long, I couldn't hear your name without recoiling. I could feel the venom rise in me, and it was horrid. I hated that you still had the ability to do that to me and be so present without physically being in my life. I'm not sure why you felt the need to do the things you did or to say the things you said. It's taken me a really long time to understand it. You made me feel unworthy of love, and I doubted myself over and over for years. It's taken a lot of people and a lot of talking to realize that your actions weren't a reflection on me, but on you. I deserve to be loved; what I didn't deserve is the pain you inflicted upon me. I'm not sure what made you act in such a horrible way. I hope that somewhere along the line you realize that, however much you attacked me, it will never fight off the demons you have. I hope one day you make peace with them, you will be a better person because of it.

Jodi

WRITE A LETTER...

to someone who changed you for the better

Some people come along and change everything. There have been people in my world who, although they've only been around for moments, have changed how I view things or how I feel about myself, and it's those people I look back on. I'm truly thankful I had them in my world, even if it was only for a little while. Write a letter to the person who changed you for the better.

Dear Alex,

You make me feel capable of achieving things that I used to shrug off as dreams, and I'm so grateful for that. Being around you gives me a strength I wish I could bottle and take a sip of whenever I'm feeling unsure of myself. It's electric! You make me feel like the very best version of myself. You have an amazing quality of being able to lift others up; you genuinely believe in people, rally behind them and support them wholeheartedly, without any agenda, and it's magic. You are magic, and you bring so much light to the worlds of those around you, and I know you don't always see that, so I'm here to remind you — my world is a much better place and I'm a better person for having you in my life. I'm forever thankful for your strength, support, wildness, whimsy and love.

Thank you,
Jodi

to the person who made you question yourself

Sometimes we meet someone who puts a spanner in the works and it makes us question something about ourselves that we've never shone a light on before. Whether it was a positive or negative experience for you, write a letter to the person who made you question yourself.

to a change-maker

Now more than ever, we have people wanting to make a change. People who want to make the world a fairer place and fight injustice are standing up and demanding to be heard. It's a time for change. Write a letter to a change-maker, whether it be someone at the UN or on your local council, who you believe in and who you really think could make a difference.

to someone in a different country

Absence makes the heart grow fonder! Write a letter to someone who lives in a different country. If everyone you know is in this country, why don't you find someone to write to via the international pen-friend association (www.ipfworld.com). You never know who you may meet and perhaps you'll make a friend for life!

To Kim,

I understand Canada has many wonderful things going for it: Justin Trudeau seems to know what he's doing, the people are lovely, the country is beautiful and your incredible family are there.

HOWEVER, everything seems a little less bright without you here. Sometimes we are lucky to meet a person that our heart recognizes straight away, almost like we'd met before in another life — we fell in love immediately. You became a big sister, loving abundantly but also not afraid to call 'Rubbish!' when you thought I wasn't being true to myself. I lost myself for quite a while, and you came with torches, roaring fire and neon signs to guide me home. I'm forever grateful for that. I know my world will always be a little less bright without you down the street, but I know that, whenever I'm feeling a little lost, it will be your signs, all that fire and all the torches you lit up in me that will guide me home. You're one of the greatest people I've ever known and I feel so lucky to have you in my world.

I love you for ever and beyond that.
Jodi

to someone who has helped you

Every day, people save lives, change lives and enhance lives as part of their jobs. They don't expect a thank you because it's in their job description, but it's always lovely to remind someone of how wonderful they are. Write a letter to someone who has helped you as part of their job.

To Mel, Sinead and Tina (and all the other lovely midwives on Ward 1 at Birmingham Women's Hospital),

I just want to let you know how incredible you are, how at ease you make women feel at their most vulnerable, and what an amazing quality that is. You brought reassurance and comfort to me at a time when I felt completely out of my depth. You were always there with a smile, ready to fix things. As women, we feel that we have to be glowing and grateful, constantly, during pregnancy, and that anything less is just unacceptable. You taught me that it's okay to find it hard when things aren't straightforward, to accept comfort without feeling like a baby and to always accept extra biscuits and the good pillows. For all that you do, for every woman you look after – thank you. You're superheroes, and I for one am very grateful you chose to be a midwife. You are simply magnificent at it.

Thanks again, for everything,
Jodi

to ask for advice

Keeping in touch by writing a letter is such an intimate way of talking to someone. I'm sure Nancy has appreciated the care and thought you've put into this project. Tell Nancy about something that has been going on in your world and ask for her advice, as she will have experienced it all before and maybe has some insight for you.

to congratulate yourself

We don't give ourselves enough credit sometimes; we skip over the good bits and focus on the bad. And sometimes we forget entirely all the amazing stuff we've been up to. Write a letter to congratulate yourself. Maybe you could write something you've achieved for each year you've been alive. Include the tiny victories and the big wins, but remind yourself that you're doing a great job.

to someone who is no longer with you

We sometimes don't get the choice to say what we'd like to say to someone. To give them a last hug or have a final phone call. Life can be incredibly cruel sometimes and steal those we love without us getting any closure at all. Use this space to write a letter to somebody who is no longer with you, in whatever way that might be.

to a historical figure

Throughout history, there have been some really incredible folk and also some terribly awful ones. Has there been anyone who you hugely admire or someone you've got a bone to pick with? Write a letter to a historical figure.

WRITE A LETTER...

to someone you are proud of

Watching someone you love go through a trying time can be excruciating, but watching them overcome it fills you with a sense of admiration and pride like no other. Here, write to someone you love who has overcome adversity. Let them know what it means to you.

To Jake,

As children, I remember being incredibly protective of you. I had a strong sense that I had to look after you – that was part of my job as a big sister. As we got older, we bumped heads a lot, due to my lack of understanding of what you were going through. I thought it was a choice and not something you had to battle with. There isn't a how-to guide on loving somebody with ADHD and autism, but I feel as though I loved you wrong, that I loved you with my ears closed a lot of the time, and I'm really sorry about that. The second you got angry because you couldn't process something I'd switch off, because I'm scared of conflicts too, which meant we never really got to solve anything. But I'm so proud of you. I write it in every birthday and Christmas card, and I'd write it on billboards if they would let me. To get to this point, this moment, you've had to jump over so many hurdles. And any time you've got into a hole, you've climbed right back out of it. For that, I am so proud of you. I am as proud now as when we first tackled your shoelaces and got rid of the Velcro — I'd never been a prouder older sister than right then. Since then, I've just become more intent on wanting to look after you — I just didn't know how at the time. Now, though, I'm loving you with my ears open.

You're so much better than you know,
Jodi

to thank a public servant

Maybe it's the lollipop person or the friendly bus driver. Maybe it's your brave local fire brigade or the guy who picks up litter. Write to someone who dedicates themselves to a public service and express your gratitude.

to someone you've hurt

Sometimes, we really mess up and hurt someone with our actions or our words. Use this space to write a letter of explanation to someone you've deeply hurt, explaining how you feel and possibly even why it happened. Maybe this isn't one you should send or, on the other hand, maybe it's the most important letter to send. Either way, be honest, be humble and be yourself.

To J,

We'd been friends since we were teenagers, we met under club lights and spent our evenings talking boys and sorting out the world's problems. I admired your ability to shut people down; you didn't allow anyone who brought drama or negativity and you could close someone's toxicity down in an instant. Something I could never do! I'm not sure why I snapped at you, why I threw the word 'crazy' out like some pre-schooler who didn't understand the connotations of it. I understood what 'crazy' referred to; I also know, if it was said to me, I'd take it the hardest, because I spend so much time trying to hide the parts of me that I deem 'crazy'. We landed ourselves in an argument about who was crazier, what people thought of the other person, and it escalated to a place of no return. And for what?

Honestly, if I could go back and have that argument again, I would call you stubborn and brash and you could have laid into me, back to a point where we wouldn't speak for a night, and

I would send a heart emoji in the morning. I loved your 'crazy', and to throw it at you as an insult was awful, and I'm so sorry for that. I panicked. I didn't know what to say, so I went for the throat before you did. It was a stupid argument. I wish it hadn't happened. We were really good friends.
I miss you.

Jodi

to someone you only know via the internet

The internet has opened our lives to a whole world of human beings who we will never come across in real life. We can now become friends with someone on the other side of the world by communicating on social media alone and create life-long friendships/instagram crushes/small obsessions. Write an IRL letter to someone you only know via the internet.

to the moment

Where are you right now? How are you feeling? What are you wearing, and is it comfy? What's making you happy? Are you excited about something? Is something worrying you? Write a letter to the moment, giving yourself a bit of an MOT. Check in with yourself and your emotions and find out where your head's at.

to someone you admire

The world is full of incredible human beings doing incredible things, but the ones with the most attention focused on them have the possibility of inspiring the greatest number of others. Write a letter to someone you admire who is in the limelight. Tell them why you admire them.

To Miranda July,

I have always tried to get into art. I have stared aimlessly at paintings and sculptures, trying to feel something, and I have been immensely jealous of anybody who does. It's made me feel stupid and embarrassed when, in a group of people discussing the most recent exhibition, I wasn't able to experience the same passion or interest. Art has never felt as if it included me. And then I came across yours. When I first read LEARNING TO LOVE YOU MORE, I felt included for the first time. It was as if I was finally being let in on a big secret — I finally got it. I read it from cover to cover and then back again. It was a story, a tapestry of human beings and their feelings, and I loved it. I read NOBODY BELONGS HERE MORE THAN YOU, and then lent it to everybody I loved because it was such a joy. I watched interviews and followed your work and, with each piece, I became more invested. I understand now that I don't have to be inspired by every single piece of art I see to have a passion for art. You made me feel included, and I'm so grateful for that. Never stop making!

Jodi

to someone you disagree with

Sometimes it feels that the most offensive and narrow-minded people have the loudest voices. But the pen is mightier than the sword! Write a letter to somebody in the spotlight who you don't admire, or who you disagree with, explaining why.

with no words

Sometimes there aren't any words. So take a picture, a piece of fabric, a part of a place you both loved or a symbol that only the two of you would understand. I'm going to send a ticket stub from when me and my best friend, Musa, went to surprise a friend of ours at his gig in New York. We'd planned it for weeks and ended up having the most amazing adventure. That ticket stub symbolizes that trip, and only Musa would get it. Write a letter with no words at all but find a way to say something.

somebody a poem

I've always written poems. Some poems sat well on paper, whereas others needed to be said out loud. Either way, I find it incredibly rewarding. You can discover poetry everywhere, in overheard conversations, a piece of art, the walk home from work or the silence before you fall asleep. Write somebody a poem.

in the form of a collage

Write a letter to someone in the form of a collage. It can be for someone's birthday, a celebration or just to cheer someone up. Get your craft box out and make something as beautiful as possible.

in one sentence

You don't have to write something long to get your point across to somebody; sometimes, a sentence will do. It took me five years to get over a boyfriend. It was a constant to and fro; every time I thought I was over him, he'd only have to look my way and I was broken-hearted again. It took me for ever – until the last time he tried to come back into my life. It didn't go the way he wanted, and he didn't like that he no longer had me on a string. My letter is for him. Write a letter to someone that sums up everything you want to say in one sentence.

To Alex,
You told me you hoped I would never be happy;
I have never been happier.

Jodi

to me

You wrote to me at the start of this book and now we're at the end. I'd love to hear from you again. Why don't you write a letter about your experience of the book and how writing letters has made you feel? Has it been therapeutic? Have you sent any? Did it make you uncomfortable or did it bring you a feeling of release? Did you enjoy your letter-writing experience? Will letters become a part of your life? What was the best letter you received in return? Get writing! That address again is:

Jodi Ann Bickley
Penguin Random House UK
80 Strand
London WC2R 0RL

This section of the book provides space for you to write your letters. Simply write, tear them out and send them! You can keep a record of who you sent them to on the stub. And place all the letters you receive in the pouch at the back for safekeeping. Enjoy.

To

To

To

To

To

To ....

To

To

To

To